I See Fall Leaves

by Mari Schuh

first step nonfiction

Lerner Publications ◆ Minneapolis

LERNER

SOURCE™

Expand learning beyond the printed book. Download free, complementary educational resources for this book from our website, www.lernerresource.com.

The images in this book are used with the permission of: © Alexey Losevich/Shutterstock.com, p. 4; © Aleksei Potov/Shutterstock.com, p. 5; © 24Novembers/Shutterstock.com, p. 6; © Belu Gheorghe/Shutterstock.com, p. 7; © leungchopan/Shutterstock.com, p. 8; © iStockphoto.com/noticelj, p. 9; © kukuruxa/Shutterstock.com, p. 10; © Nadiia Korol/Shutterstock.com, p. 11; © iStockphoto.com/Ivanna Reznichenko, p. 12; © orangecrush/Shutterstock.com, p. 13; © iStockphoto.com/Viktor_Kitaykin, p. 14; © iStockphoto.com/ Denice Breaux, p. 15; © Josie Elias/Getty Images, p. 16; © iStockphoto.com/photosbyash, p. 17; © LWA/Dan Tardif/Getty Images, p. 18; © Blue Jean Images/Getty Images, p. 19; © Ariel Skelley/Getty Images, p. 20; © MaszaS/Shutterstock.com, p. 21; © Sergey Novikov/Shutterstock.com, p. 22. Front cover: © saraporn/Shutterstock.com.

Main body text set in ITC Avant Garde Gothic Std Medium 21/25. Typeface provided by International Typeface Corp.

Lerner Publications Company
A division of Lerner Publishing Group, Inc.
241 First Avenue North
Minneapolis, MN 55401 USA

For reading levels and more information, look up this title at www.lernerbooks.com.

Library of Congress Cataloging-in-Publication Data

Schuh, Mari C., 1975– author.
    I see fall leaves / by Mari Schuh.
        pages cm. — (First step nonfiction. Observing fall)
    Audience: Ages 5–8.
    Audience: K to grade 3.
    Summary: "This title examines different properties of fall leaves, including such things as color and texture. Readers will learn to observe the world around them as well as to spot signs of seasonal changes in nature"— Provided by publisher.
    Includes index.
    ISBN 978-1-5124-0795-2 (lb : alk. paper) — ISBN 978-1-5124-1215-4 (pb : alk. paper) — ISBN 978-1-5124-0996-3 (eb pdf)
    1. Leaves—Juvenile literature. 2. Leaves—Color—Juvenile literature. 3. Autumn—Juvenile literature. I. Title.
QK649.S3584 2016
575.5'7—dc23   2015033942

Manufactured in the United States of America
1 – CG – 7/15/16

Table of Contents

Fall Leaves

It is fun to look at leaves in the **fall**.

Look at all the colorful leaves on the ground!

Leaves change color in the fall.

Leaves can turn yellow.

Leaves can turn orange.

Some maple leaves are red.

Leaves can turn red.

Leaves can turn brown too.

Parts and Shapes

These leaves are hanging by their stems.

Leaves have **stems**.

The yellow lines in these leaves are veins.

Leaves have **veins**.

These long leaves are willow leaves.

Some leaves are long and **narrow**.

Some leaves are **oval**.

Some leaves are round
and wide.

White oak
leaves are curvy.

Some leaves are curvy.

Some leaves are shaped
like hearts.

Sweet gum leaves have a star shape.

Some leaves are shaped like stars.

Leaves drop from trees.

They are dry and crunchy.

People rake leaves.

People play in leaves too.

Collecting leaves can be fun!

What can you do with fall leaves?

Glossary

fall – the season between summer and winter

narrow – not wide

oval – a shape that is curved, like an egg

stems – the thin parts of a plant from which leaves grow

veins – thin, stiff tubes inside a leaf

Index